Jeeps

Thomas Streissguth

Capstone Press

MINNEAPOLIS

Printed in the United States of America.

Capstone Press • 2440 Fernbrook Lane • Minneapolis, MN 55447

Editorial Director   John Coughlan
Managing Editor   John Martin
Production Editor   James Stapleton

Library of Congress Cataloging-in-Publication Data

Streissguth, Thomas, 1958-
   Jeeps / by Thomas Streissguth
      p. cm. -- (Cruisin')
   Includes bibliographical references and index.
   ISBN 1-56065-255-1 : $13.35
   1. Jeep automobile--Juvenile literature.
[1. Jeep automobile.] I. Title. II. Series
TL215.J44S77 1996
629.22'042--dc20   95-7128
                                                         CIP
                                                         AC

99 98 97 96 95   6   5   4   3   2   1

Table of Contents

Chapter 1

Going Off-Road

It's a cold, windy day. You're driving a smooth, two-lane highway in the mountains of British Columbia. There are no towns, no gas stations, and not much traffic.

Up ahead are sheer cliffs, steep hills, and a dense forest of fir trees. The road leads straight through the trees and between the hills. The **shoulders** are muddy from last night's rain. There's only one road in sight.

You spot a thin trail leading away from the road. There are no signs or markings. Two ruts in the ground show you where the wheels of other vehicles have passed before.

The four-wheel-drive jeep, a vehicle with a long history, can still handle rough roads and tough conditions.

You're not sure where this track leads. But you decide to take it anyway. You engage the **four-wheel drive**, and your vehicle leaps into the narrow ruts. Suddenly, you're off-road.

Your wheels take the bumps and dips with ease. You make sharp turns across the rough ground without slowing down. The powerful motor revs up for the steep hillsides. You climb with the front end pointed almost straight up.

A Vehicle with a Story

You're driving a Jeep Wrangler. This is not just another **sport-utility vehicle**. The story of the jeep goes back more than 50 years.

The jeep was the original sport-utility vehicle. Its builders designed the first jeeps for service in World War II. Many people think the jeep played a big part in winning that war.

Chapter 2

The Birth of the Jeep

It was the summer of 1940. In Europe, the armies of Germany were on the march. They were fighting in France, Holland, Denmark, and Norway. England was expecting a German invasion.

The United States was not yet fighting. But the Army knew that it would have to prepare quickly. The military would soon need new guns, tanks, and artillery.

The Army also needed an entirely new kind of vehicle. Officers wanted a small, all-purpose car with four-wheel drive. This car would have to be durable and easy to repair. It would also

American Bantam built this prototype of the general-purpose (GP) car for the U.S. Army in 1940.

have to go across rugged terrain under the worst conditions.

The Army invited 135 manufacturers to send plans for a new "general-purpose" car. Time was short. Only American Bantam Car

Company and Willys-Overland Motors, Inc. responded.

The Race Is On

American Bantam hired the engineer Karl Probst to draw up plans for a vehicle. Probst finished a set of drawings in five days. By September 23, 1940, the first American Bantam **prototype**s were built and ready for testing.

The Quad wasn't pretty, but it was good enough for the U.S. Army. Willys modeled the MB jeep after it.

The car, named the BRC (Bantam **Reconnaissance** Car) 40, pleased Army officials. But they didn't think that American Bantam, a small company, could produce enough cars in time.

So the military allowed both Willys-Overland and the Ford Motor Company to copy Bantam's plans. Both of these companies then produced their own prototypes. Willys-Overland executives named their car the Quad. Ford called its general-purpose prototype the Pygmy.

Each of the three models had an outstanding feature. The Willys engine, called the Go-Devil, was the most powerful. The Pygmy had good steering. Bantam's model used less fuel than the other two.

In November 1940, the Army ordered 1,500 vehicles from each of the three companies for further testing. When Army officials finally made their decision, they named Willys the main supplier. Ford would also build the cars. American Bantam was out of luck.

After World War II, civilians bought new jeep models, such as this Jeepster, for more peaceful uses.

The MB, the GPW, and the Jeep

Willys named the new general-purpose vehicle the Willys MB. Ford named its version the GPW (General-Purpose Willys). Soldiers called these new vehicles Peeps, Beetle Bugs,

Midgets, Leaping Lenas, or Puddle Jumpers. But everyone called them jeeps, from GP (general-purpose) vehicle.

The car had two seats in front and a bench seat in the rear. A 15-gallon (56.8-liter) gas tank gave it a range of 298 miles (480 kilometers). Top speed was 67 miles (104 kilometers) per hour. Between the seats was a

Interiors have changed over the years, and civilian Jeeps are much more comfortable than military versions.

Its simple design and low weight allowed the military jeep to go anywhere.

mount for a .30-caliber Browning machine gun. The entire unit cost the Army about $900.

The Willys MB had storage bins in the rear and a rack for gas cans in the back. There were brackets for an ax and shovel on the side. Grab handles on the sides of the car allowed cranes to lift the jeep. For an airdrop, soldiers could attach parachutes to these handles.

The jeep had no doors. Instead, cutaway sides allowed soldiers to climb in and out quickly. In case of bad weather, there was also a canvas top. A double-paned windshield protected the driver and passengers from flying rocks and dust. The driver or a passenger had to move the windshield wipers back and forth by hand.

The jeep had one other important feature. With about an hour's work, soldiers could waterproof it. They covered the electrical system—battery, starter, and other parts—with waterproof grease. Then they added a long exhaust pipe that rose above the sides of the jeep. This allowed jeeps to cross rivers and deep streams. Jeeps were often the first vehicles ashore during sea-borne landings.

The Common Jeep

Ford and Willys made more than 600,000 jeeps during World War II. There were **amphibious** models, which the soldiers called "seeps." "Fleeps" were lightweight jeeps made

This postwar jeep may have seen action in the Korean War or in Vietnam.

for airdrops. There were also ambulance jeeps and tractor jeeps. Drivers could replace the jeep's regular rubber tires with steel wheels for use on railroad tracks.

This family of jeeps includes (from left to right) the Quad prototype, the Willys MB, the M38A1, and the M606A2.

By the end of World War II, jeeps were crowding the cities, roads, and fields of Europe. There were plenty of jeeps to go around. There were so many of them, in fact, that there was usually no need for soldiers to use the back seat.

Once, a group of German spies crossed into United States-held territory in a captured jeep.

The Germans wore United States uniforms, carried American weapons, and spoke perfect English. But they made one mistake. They crowded four passengers into a single jeep. American military police (MPs) spotted them easily, and the mission failed. The MPs knew that four American soldiers would have had at least two jeeps to use.

Chapter 3

Postwar Jeeps

World War II ended in 1945. The United States Army still found the jeep useful for general transportation. Many jeeps also found their way into **civilian** hands. Thousands more ended up in the armies of other countries.

New and Improved Jeeps

After the war, the United States Army needed a new and improved jeep. In 1949 Willys designed the MC jeep. It was slightly taller than the Willys MB jeep. An important improvement was its windshield, made out of a single pane of glass for better visibility.

In 1954, the Willys MD jeep appeared. The United States Army called it the M-38A1. With 72 **horsepower**, the four-**cylinder** engine was slightly more powerful than the Willys MBs used during World War II.

Willys designed another new jeep, the M151, in 1959. The United States Army called this vehicle the Mutt, for Military Utility Tactical Truck. The M151 had four-wheel independent suspension, higher horsepower, and a four-speed transmission. But the Mutt was easy to roll and dangerous on hills and curves.

The rollover problem was so serious that the Army destroyed **surplus** Mutts rather than sell them to the public. This has made the original Mutt a rare collector's item.

The M422, known as the Mighty Mite, was in production from 1960 until 1963. Willys designed this vehicle especially for the United States Marines. Its body was aluminum, instead of steel. This made the vehicle lighter and quicker. During the Vietnam War (1963-1974),

Some postwar military models, such as this M151, had a horizontal front grille.

the Mighty Mite saw a lot of action under tough conditions.

These post-World War II jeeps had a wide range of uses. Some carried anti-tank missiles instead of machine guns. Others had battlefield radar on board. The military used jeeps to lay

For safety, manufacturers designed new roll bars and an enclosed cab for civilian Jeeps.

telephone wire, carry prisoners, and perform reconnaissance missions.

A New Kind of General-Purpose Vehicle

In 1979 the Army decided it needed a general-purpose vehicle with an entirely new design. This was the High Mobility Multi-Purpose Wheeled Vehicle, or Humvee. AM

General Company of Mishawaka, Indiana, began producing these vehicles in 1985.

The Humvee is a tough vehicle that can go over any kind of terrain. A low center of gravity makes it almost impossible to roll. The diesel engine has eight cylinders and puts out 150 horsepower.

The Humvee has replaced the jeep as the general-purpose military vehicle of the United States Army. But thousands of civilians and military personnel around the world still drive jeeps. And collectors are restoring many of the World War II jeeps to their original condition. One of the toughest vehicles ever made, the jeep lives on.

Chapter 4

Civilian Jeeps

After World War II, the jeep began a new career as a civilian vehicle. Willys-Overland **patented** the name "jeep" and turned it into a brand name–Jeep. The company designed a new version for use in peacetime. It sold this civilian Jeep as a farm tractor, a fire engine, a hauler, and an ambulance.

The first civilian Jeep was the CJ-2A. Willys designed it with the same 60-horsepower engine, the same 80-inch (203-centimeter) **wheelbase**, and the same **leaf-spring suspension** as the wartime jeeps had.

The company added a **tailgate** and larger headlights. They mounted the spare tire on the side, instead of the rear. A reflector on the right rear replaced the right taillight.

Farmers, mail carriers, and construction crews put the CJ-2A to work. But in the late 1940s, the general public was not very interested in owning one. Most people wanted big, comfortable cars.

The Jeepster

In 1948, Willys introduced the Jeepster. This was a sporty version of the civilian Jeep. It had a canvas top and **sidecurtains** that drivers could raise or lower. It cost $1,885—expensive for a car in 1948. Willys offered either the Go-Devil four-cylinder engine or the Lightning six-cylinder engine on its Jeepsters. The car also had independent front suspension for a smooth ride.

The Jeepster's unusual look didn't attract many buyers. Willys built only 19,000 of them. In 1950, the company discontinued the line.

The Jeepster convertible had wide whitewall tires, a roomy back seat, and the classic jeep front-end design.

Because few are around today, an original Jeepster in good condition is a rare and valuable collector's car.

New Engines, New Jeeps

Willys introduced the CJ-3B in 1952. Its Hurricane F-Head engine put out 75 horsepower. Three years later, the CJ-5, or Universal Jeep, introduced a new look. It had rounded front fenders.

In 1967, the Kaiser Company brought back the classic Jeepster of 1948. The company also made convertibles, **roadsters,** pickups, and station wagons under the name Jeepster Commando. They looked much like Willys's CJ jeeps from the front.

In 1972, the American Motors Corporation (AMC), Kaiser's parent company, dropped the Jeepster name. The company also changed the Jeepster Commando's grille to look more like a regular passenger car's front. Sales fell, and the Commando line was discontinued the next year.

Jeeps of the 1980s

In the 1970s, sport-utility vehicles became popular. Many people wanted to travel off-road, over unmarked trails. Some bought the Jeep CJ-6, which first rolled off the assembly

The Jeep Wrangler became one of the leaders in the growing sport-utility market.

line in 1980. This jeep was long, with a wheelbase of 101 inches (256 centimeters).

As sales increased, the Jeep CJ-6 offered new luxury options. Off-road drivers could

travel in style, with carpeting, air conditioning, power steering, and power brakes.

Meanwhile, the Willys-Overland company was going through changes. Part of Kaiser-Frazer since the early 1950s, the Jeep division

was sold to American Motors Corporation in 1970. In 1987, the Chrysler Corporation bought the Jeep division when it purchased American Motors.

Chapter 5
Jeeps for Fun

By the 1980s, four-wheel-drive vehicles were no longer just for work. Many people wanted a rugged car that could go anywhere–even cross-country.

The CJ-7 jeeps appeared first in 1976. They were the first jeeps with automatic transmissions. With a 304-cubic-inch V-8 engine and a Quadra-Trac four-wheel drive, the CJ-7 could travel over all kinds of roads as well as unmarked tracks. It was one of the best off-road vehicles available.

There were several different versions of the CJ-7 jeep. One, the Laredo, offered a shiny

chrome grille, bumpers, and wheels. It also had **cruise control**, a stereo radio, and air conditioning.

A Brand New Jeep–The AMC Wrangler

American Motors Corporation ended the CJ jeep line in 1986. The decision made many

Driving off-road can be dangerous. Jeep designers added roll bars to protect the driver in case of a rollover.

people angry. They did not want to see the classic jeep pass into history.

The Wrangler replaced the CJ jeep. Its design was close to that of the earliest jeeps. Instead of round lamps, however, it had rectangular headlights. It also boasted a smoother ride and better handling. In Canada, the Wrangler is known as the YJ.

The Wrangler's standard engine was a 150-cubic-inch, four-cylinder engine that made 121 horsepower. A six-cylinder engine was optional. Buyers could choose a hard top or a canvas top.

The Wrangler, like the CJ jeep, had a roll bar. But American Motors Corporation added another set of bars that ran from the windshield back to the roll bar. This gave the passenger compartment extra protection in case of a rollover.

Chrysler still makes Wranglers. The Wrangler S and Rio Grande models have 123-horsepower, 2.5-liter engines. The SE, Sport, and Sahara models of the Wrangler have the most powerful engine in the sport-utility class—a 180-horsepower, 4.0-liter engine. The Wrangler is the modern version of the jeep—and still one of the best ways to go off-road.

Glossary

amphibious–able to float or move through water

civilian–not belonging to the military

cruise control–a device that automatically keeps a vehicle moving at a steady speed

cylinder–an engine chamber where fuel is burned

four-wheel drive–a system linking the engine directly to all four wheels, instead of just two

horsepower–a measure of engine strength. One horsepower equals the strength to move 500 pounds (227 kilograms) one foot (30.5 centimeters) per second.

leaf-spring suspension–a series of metal strips that supports a vehicle and helps prevent damage from uneven roads

patent–to register a name or invention so that others may not use it without permission

prototype–a full-scale model built for testing

reconnaissance–a search of enemy territory

roadster–a term for an open touring car with a folding top

shoulders–the sides of a road, usually built of gravel or sand

sidecurtains–windshields that can be removed with a convertible top

sport-utility vehicle–a vehicle designed for use on a variety of roads and over open ground

surplus–extra material that is no longer needed

tailgate–a door on the back of a vehicle

wheelbase–the length from front to rear axles, giving a measure of the size of a vehicle

To Learn More

Fowler, Will. *Jeep Goes to War: A Pictorial Chronicle*. Philadelphia: Courage Books, 1993.

Guttmacher, Peter. *Jeep*. New York: Crestwood House, 1994.

Sessler, Peter C. *Illustrated Jeep Buyer's Guide*. Osceola, Wisconsin: Motorbooks International, 1988.

Smith, Jay H. *Humvees and Other Military Vehicles*. Minneapolis: Capstone Press, 1994.

Photo Credits

Chrysler Motors: pgs. 12, 13, 15, 16-17, 18, 19, 21, 22-23, 27, 33, 35, 42

Petersen Publishing: pgs. 4, 6-7, 8, 10, 24, 28, 30, 36-37, 38, 40-41

Index